Outside the Calendar

Kjell Espmark

Outside the Calendar

Selected Poems

translated by Robin Fulton Macpherson

LIBRARY OF CONGRESS CATALOGUING
IN PUBLICATION DATA
Espmark, Kjell
Poems. Selected Poems. English. Translations.
Outside the Calendar: Selected Poems/ Kjell Espmark;
translated from the Swedish by Robin Fulton Macpherson.
ISBN: 978-1-934851-38-8

Copyright © 1968, 1972, 1975, 1979, 1982, 1984, 1992, 1998,
2002, 2007 by Kjell Espmark
Translation Copyright © 2012 by Robin Fulton Macpherson
and Kjell Espmark

Design and typesetting by HSDesigns
Cover design by HSDesigns
Printed and bound in the United States.

Marick Press
P.O. Box 36253
Grosse Pointe Farms
Michigan 48236
www.marickpress.com

Distributed by spdbooks.org and Ingram

MARICK PRESS

TRANSLATOR'S NOTE:

I have been translating Kjell Espmark's poems, on and off, for about 35 years, and this book is a selection of our efforts. I say "our" because these versions resulted from close cooperation and I owe much to the poet's patience and helpfulness. If any reader finds the English here disagreeable, they will have to blame the translator and not the poet.

—RFM

Contents

Minns Du   10
Do You Remember   11

from *Det offentliga samtalet / Voices in Public* (1968):
In the Hospital It's Two O'Clock   15
When the Earth Was Still Open   17
Made in Sweden   18

from *Samtal under jorden / Voices under Ground* (1972)
The Emigrants   20
It Must Be Tiresias' House   22
He's Sitting on a Bench in the Past   23

from *Det obevekliga paradiset / The Inexorable Paradise* (1975)
Beside Her Desk Is *the Desk*   24
The Director of the Environment's Secret Journey   26
The Deceived One: Only a Feeble Outline   28
They Don't Even Take Shelter   30

from *Försök till liv / Attempts at Life* (1979)
Pastoral   35
Family Gathering   39
The Royal Library, October 4th   44

from *Tecken till Europa / Signs of Europe* (1982)
The Cathedral in Chartres   47
Escorial   50
The Time of the Great War   54

    Béla Bartók against the Third Reich   57

from *Den hemliga måltiden / The Secret Meal* (1984)
    A Book to Burn   60
    I´m Still Called Osip Mandelstam   63
    The Imperial Army in Xían   66
    The First Shadow in the Wall   69

from *När vägen vänder / Route Tournante* (1992)
    When a Language Dies   75
    How Wrong, Yet How Persistent…   76
    Sunday at Museo Frida Kahlo   77
    Prague Quartet   79
    from Jotted on History´s Margin   84
    Four Greek Voices From Under the Ground   86
    Impromptu   89
    Outside the Calendar   90
    From Illuminations   91
    Route Tournante   92

from *Det andra livet / The Other Life* (1998)
    The Other Life   94
    The Day We Buried Foucault   96
    Life for Sale   98
    Caribbean Quartet   100
    Letter Writing   104
    Family Memory   105
    Archetype   106

from *De levande har inga gravar /
The Living Have No Graves* (2002)
    Didn´t You Tell Me a Dream   107
    I Knew That Photos Faded   108
    Hold Me Tight So I Don´t Flee   109
    Vita Nuova   110
    If Even Denied a Mayfly´s Hour   111
    Silence   112

from *Vintergata / Lend Me Your Voice* (2007)
    Introduction to *Lend Me Your Voice*   117
    Although an Ice Block Has Saved Me for Your Time   118
    The Air Smells of Approaching Thunder   119
    I Was Standing in Front of Anubis   120
    It Was Plague Month in Athens   121
    When I Had Stopped Breathing   122
    It Must Have Been a Hall   123
    My Horsemen Had Conquered the World   124
    I Was Called Maria   125
    In the Minutes Before They Fetched Me   126
    As in Earlier Years   127
    We'd Been Driven in Chains along the Paths   128
    Driving My Load across the Ice   129
    All I Owned Was a Sledge-hammer   130
    I Think I Took to Preaching   131
    One of a Swarm He Leapt at the Trench   132
    I Stooped along the Dark Passage   133
    An Arrested Moment in a Garden   134
    Lying in My Cell   135
    On That Day the Gods Took the Shape   136
    Before Sinking onto the Bench   137

About the Author   139

MINNS DU

Minns du den grekiska gravreliefen—
ett avsked av sten:
den ena ska just gå förlorad i stenen,
den andra stanna i sitt halva liv.
Svårt att se var de två gestalterna
ska kunna skiljas åt. Den enas hand
är ju en del av den andras höft,
den enas böjda huvud ett stycke
av den andras skakande skuldra.
Denna stund måste vara
inte bara den döendes avsked
från det liv som gnistrar i stenen
och den levandes rop efter delen som dör
utan också ett avsked från den andras sinnen
och den andras ilande minnen,
från det lånade öga man såg igenom
och det liv den andra levt i en.
Den som just har dött
dröjer ett tidlöst ögonblick
under ett böljande lövverk av sten
för att trösta den som blev kvar.

DO YOU REMEMBER

Do you remember the Greek grave relief—
a leave-taking in stone:
the one is about to be lost in the stone,
the other to stay in a half life.
Hard to see where the figures
could be separated. The one's hand
is a part of the other's thigh,
the one's bowed head a piece
of the other's trembling shoulder.
This moment must be
not only the leave-taking of the dying
from the life that sparkles in the stone
and the cry of the living for the part that is dying,
but also a leave-taking from the other's senses
and the other's quick memories,
from the borrowed eye one saw through
and the life the other lived in one.
The one who has just died
lingers a timeless moment
under a billowing foliage of stone
to comfort the one who is left.

LATE IN SWEDEN

from *Det offentliga samtalet / Voices in Public*
(1968)

from *Samtal under jorden / Voices under Ground*
(1972)

from *Det obevekliga paradiset / The Inexorable Paradise*
(1975)

IN THE HOSPITAL IT´S TWO O´CLOCK

Enter the room, double.
Hover at the bedside, double.
"Someone to see you, Herr Ancker!"
A groan among the blanket´s flakes.
Motionless on the bed, eyes closed, the invalid
rises towards the visitor
gropes over cheeks and clothes
tries to assemble it all
into something he recognizes.
The nurse strokes the blanket: "Herr Ancker!"
Laboriously he faces outwards
extricates a grin from the sheet:
"Well, if it isn´t you!"
His head is shaved, rubber tubes and horns of glass.
"It´s long since."
The echo carries through neglected years.
"What lovely strawberries you´ve brought!"
Fingering the grapes.
The room throbs to his headache.
"I see you double, you know."

Motionless on the bed
he´s standing at the window
staring down at his divided Stockholm:
in winter light two fragile cities
which have glided a handsbreadth apart.
Spires emerging from spires
crowds hurrying out of themselves.

"What lovely strawberries."
The visitor´s heart rattles, double and dry.
The language the invalid´s fumbling in
echoes with childhood summers.
"That was nice of you."
It´s not much he wants:

a window that doesn´t glide out of the window
a hand that remains in itself.
Content with five centimetres´ coherence
at eye-level.
It´s denied him.

WHEN THE EARTH WAS STILL OPEN

A blackened corner of the cemetery
already bears its cross: Henrik Ancker, lost.
Each one alone in driving snow.
Divided, a handsbreadth behind themselves
the mourners stand round this black box
that refuses to sink in the earth
hangs in the air
while the clods tumble in the pit.
He actually leans over the edge
grabs the priest´s collar and refuses!
They try persuasion, a frozen mumbling.
He pretends to agree to the ceremony.
But then when everything´s said or unsaid
and they shake hands and part
he keeps them company
this way and that
not really much thinner
than those who are trying to mourn him.

MADE IN SWEDEN

Morning. Grey. Eternal winter.
Keep still, boy, and let me reach.
The milk will soon freeze in its glass.

Sh! Not so loud.
The eyes of neighbours glare from the wallpaper.
A ten-storey conversation
through walls and floors.
The toilets roar like mighty accordions
in this peasant village balanced on end.

That quivering lower lip.
Why, aren´t you a boy:
clip clip.
The personality in rough outline
is shaped of old by sheep-shears.

You must learn loneliness.
The hand reaching for a face
should jerk – so,
like a train going through points
and off in another direction.

It´s the others that count, not you.
You´ll do what they expect of you.
Chin up!
It´s you I set my hopes on.
Me—I´ve have been cheated out of life.
Oh, these thousands and thousands of steps just for you.
Now run off to school, to life, into the stone.
Give me back my life.

He is standing in the harsh stairwell light
that has no place for hands
and smiles as always, trapped in politeness.

Has learned to be silent with his whole body.
The entire Swedish peasantry
keeps silent in him.

Conscious now of the voters around him:
there are always eyes noting everything.
You should climb in those eyes, you know.
The result doesn´t depend on who you are
but on what the others see in you.

He learns to keep such persistent silence
that his clenched teeth clench the jaws
of those around who still have jaws.

His eye is close now. It is stern,
not yet corrupt.
But his heart has learned no language.

What did you say? Nothing?
You never tell me anything.
But in his severe silence the mother reads:
I give you back your life.

THE EMIGRANTS

Do we darken the night sky for you
with our jerking procession of caravans, rusted
cars, creaking bicycles, dogs and bundles?
Do we become motes in the big telescope
with our tattered rags, grimy infants at the breast—
the unborn, behind, can´t catch up.
No, you can see the stars straight through us
through this clamorous multitude
thin as a promise
and driven away since the morning of time.
Nowhere are we allowed to burden
the cosmic community tax
or lower the value of the neighbouring villas.
Try in the next galaxy, you said.
We are trying. We reconnoitre for you.
Our timeless life
is an experiment in homelessness.
We made our way through your language.
Our hands were shaped into picklocks
by all your locked doors.
Our faces became feigned innocence
before all that suspicion.
We made our way through.
And if you hear signals on car-horns and frying-pans
from years beyond time and reason
we´ll have found a new continent for you.

With my hat over my face
I rest in the grass. It´s always with us
even among the furthest stars.
Willow-herb up through my breast. Quaking-grass.
The front of the procession
has the same colour as the darkness.
I myself am among the last.
Hear them, the steps on the gravel, squeaking wheels

the wailing of infants, all those noises
we´ve had with us, almost worn out now.
We´re trying in the next galaxy.

IT MUST BE TIRESIAS' HOUSE

I guess you want to meet the old fellow
to have a peep into the future.
It's the old errand for anyone
making his way down to us shadows.
But you must content yourself with the boards here.
We have nailed him in.
It's nothing to make a story of.
He just began talking one day
of a whiteness so intense it could be heard.
He said he could see the absurd.
What exists out there doesn't exist, he said.
It is present in the sense
that it *cannot* exist.
That thought finds no hold in one's head.
He said that he waited for ages
for the rustle of leaves.
But there were no trees there.
And the agitated murmur of men
was neither murmur nor men.
There was only a whitened moment
that went on and on
while one's body was more and more tense.
Like some kind of patience with one.
We just couldn't listen to more.
So we boarded up his raised hand
the holes that were his eyes
and the mouth that grew old as he spoke.
We consider much is achieved
if we keep him silent.

HE´S SITTING ON A BENCH IN THE PAST

for Gunnar Ekelöf

I took you for another
when you came in the burning stairway.
Your shadow looked like an axeman´s.
I am familiar with the axe, you see.
Had it day after day in my throat
a prolonged beheading. Month after month.
The executioner aimed badly, thought
I could be parted from the song all the same.
I refused.
He gave me a place here in hell while I lived.

The axe was lifted sky-high.
His neck sinews tautened like string.
His sweaty chest was trembling.
I saw Stockholm thicken round me
where I lay on the rough paving stones.
The harried crowds of Iron Square
made way for cholera-churls and soldiers,
journeymen, shop-maids, carpenters.
A city which carried its lost within itself
stood bowed over me and gave me its strength.
The axe fell.
I refused.
Never was the song more my own.

One night in March he gave up.
Now I can move freely.
As you hear from the others
my dialect is already current here.
Are the vaults too low for song, you mean?
That´s what makes song possible.
If you renounce your listening
you´ll hear the fierce music.

BESIDE HER DESK IS *THE DESK*

She's listening with her whole body.
The teacher's lips are moving. And she hears
yet misses his words by a few inches
like trying to grab a stone in water.
There's another world, a handsbreadth from hers.
Right against the map of Sweden
there hangs a map of *Sweden*—
the same towns and jagged lakes
the same yellow and green fields
yet a country shimmering and inaccessible.
They're discussing something now, their mouths in motion.
Of course she can hear. But what's really said
flies sparkling past her ears
to those living in the right country.

Yet she can catch them in the interval
with her sniffling story of daddy being picked up
struggling, pulled out every way.
And mother tried to hide herself in her hands.
Everything's sold for twenty wrinkled laughs.
Talks, straddling, stockings rumpling.

But nothing is changed by her success.
When she tries to take her place in *their* talk
she stumbles into that thin membrane
separating the world from *the world*
and that smile which hurts so much
because it's not intended to be seen.
If she could wrangle herself into their Sweden
and carefully sit down among them
would her chair not change into a *chair*
and herself become quite real?
One step to the side is all she needs.
But finds not even a word for that step.
And the classroom knows: she'll never find it.

The language between these four walls
knows her life to come.
She can struggle till she's pulled out every way.
In this amiably inexorable grammar
each has their final place.

THE DIRECTOR OF THE ENVIRONMENT´S SECRET JOURNEY

One day in September—air pressure 1005 millibar—
he makes his way down into the future
just as King Alexander in the story
was lowered into the sea in a barrel of glass
(gloomily gazing out at the huge whale
and men at pasture in the deep´s floating forests).
He must at last find out for himself
and put an end to the nuclear squabble.
While the greasy lines run out
he sees through the bottle-green glass
the two deformed assistants at the windlass
exchange a glance that makes him swallow hard
then shrink to nothing.
He has down with him some borrowed experts
who thoughtfully formulate the opinions
their place in the dialogue prescribes.
Still nothing unsettling in the world outside the glass.
The phosphorescing cities are growing
largely according to plan.
A kind of terrace, it seems.
At least the vessel stops sinking.
But what in God´s name is this!
Flat against the glass they stare into the absurd.
Faces like sparklers
now here now there.
A woman, close-to, wants to say something.
But her voice is an incomprehensible crackle.
With awkward gestures instead of hands
she seems to warn of something that can´t be seen.
She has her children around her. As if they branched out
like a mycelium, uncheckable.
The travellers are afflicted by such trembling
their understanding comes loose in its sockets.
They gasp for words.

One of them hits on a phrase—"in a wider context..."
And that saves them.
As soon as they have a tongue in their head
they can defend themselves against what they see.
Their language is a huge filter.
Now the sparkling souls outside the glass
can be allowed to witness. They´re at once simplified
to abstractions, can be recognised
as the least important values in the calculation.
A signal´s given. And the vessel rises.
Their thoughts move more nimbly.
Soon they can see their boat and its green
bubbly twisted faces
which already feel they know
the pacifying report.

THE DECEIVED ONE:
ONLY A FEEBLE OUTLINE

So she's been somebody else for eight years
without knowing it.
Every day has been a misunderstanding.
She clings to the basin. The bathroom keeps heeling over.
What's awful is not her suddenly looking
into a rapture implacable as that of insects.
What's awful is seeing, one afternoon,
eight years of her life bartered.
The children have known. And spared themselves.
This love has belonged to all her acquaintances,
a community full of swaying antennae.
Only she's been shut out.
The price of their calm, with the shimmer of beetles,
is her counterfeit existence.
She stares at the transparent face in the mirror.
It's totally alien.
Her hands turning white round the basin,
not much more than their whiteness,
are not hers. She can't keep this down.
And she throws up all her lying memories:
this dimmed face above her,
dissolved in lust and assurances,
his sudden youth—an outing in whirling snow and laughter,
these mature moments in the light round the dining-table
when his voice made the appartment real.
She throws up all this bogus life,
these days smelling of old shrimp shells.
Sitting at last on the bathroom floor,
totally destitute. Nothing left of the eight years.
Just the metal taste in her mouth.
You must give me back my years!
The children get out of the way, suddenly adult,
embarrassed by the rhetoric, by these remains of despair
that don't even have any words of their own.

And the neighbour´s eyes in the bathroom tiles!
She´s sitting bent round her aching void,
trying to hide her poverty
with her back turned to all those who knew.

THEY DON´T EVEN TAKE SHELTER

What an endless procession towards the city.
Clowns, tinkers, swindlers, ragmen,
car dealers without cars, drunkards.
The glowing walls, the inexorable towers
in the distance are growing in the thoughts of all.
The heavenly sewage-smell already reaches them
at twenty kilometres. Sweeter than honey.
What do they hope for?
Work, a bundle of straw on the floor,
half a square metre for their life?
Meaningless.
For each step they take nearer the city
they must relinquish a piece of themselves.
They belong to under-history
where not even the *word* revolt exists.
The crowd is tight and thin like a Dürer engraving.
Around them crows circle
over colourless acres, waiting.
From wheels nailed up
on the posts along the road
they hear the parching cries of those
who tried to enter glory
on their own terms.
But the migrants don´t look up.
Their muddy gaze hides
in the mud of the road.
Think with your feet! One hardly dares
even to glance at the distant walls
that must be trembling in the mist.
Each one of those pulsating bundles
counts itself worth at least
the coin we´re born with in our fist.
But demands also a place in reality.
They seem unconquerable
since the crowd will never end.

Always facing a headwind
they´re made for leaning forward.
The only colour they know is brown.
Those at the front,
approaching the merciless gates
are already walking into their invisibility.

ATTEMPTS

from *Försök till liv/Attempts at Life*
(1979)

from *Tecken till Europa/Signs of Europe*
(1982)

from *Den hemliga måltiden / The Secret Meal*
(1984)

PASTORAL

When the car swings in and the engine stops
there´s only silence, a huge white sky of silence,
plains of silence. The Baltic, close,
is breathing almost imperceptibly
through this which is not tree,
through this which is not grass
yet. The children carry a premonition,
partly rising, partly trembling.
And suddenly it´s there, the lark, still only a song
drawing the fields into hazy existence.
The first steps taken together out into emptiness
are met with a transparent gleaming,
ten centimetres high, with darker imprints:
points that change from glittering yellow to green,
from stinging red to blue when you move.
The suitcases lie in the meaningless.

The summer house, thin hovering surfaces of plaster:
a low-voiced answer in Gotland limestone.
They have longed it forth, the one an implied gable,
the other a window that rattles on its catch.
And now they´re sitting in the sun on the steps.
The razor-blade scrapes through the lather
—there is no cheek beneath—
to entice out a recognisable face.
The boy takes the mirror and sends a reflection dancing
and a piece of Svensson´s barn exists.
The girl reads in her father´s thoughts:
he´s been surprised by his early years.
The children finger this old-fashioned childhood
to define themselves. It has none of their integrity.

This boy walks in what is not yet grass, without fear
though he too knows a foot can burst through.
The girl hears the voices and the steps

under what is not yet grass, and shudders.
But both of them look the adult calmly in the eye
without his campaign strategies.
In the door a figure stands, invisible in this picture,
but the skin on one´s back feels the light coming from her.

Must get ground round the house now.
What the swinging makes into a scythe
advances in what the edge makes into grass.
The children rake with nothing in nothing.
Common labour forces
a shimmering moist green surface
to appear in wisps. With each step
a sole of meaning is gained. They secure
a fragment of summer for each other. And themselves
become visible in the midst of their creation.

The boy is averted, engaged
in restoring spiders and wood-lice.
The swallows may also have something to do
with his concentration: swoop out of nothing,
like quick rejoinders, and vanish under the eaves.
Unobserved he climbs the ash tree
that breaks into green, branch by branch, higher and higher,
and at last surrounds him gleaming
where curled in a fork
he loses himself in *The Count of Monte Cristo*.
The story he reads has just been written.

The girl reads in the walls
where the wrangling, in old spelling, lingers
half eaten away by mice
but persists, long after quarrel and memory are gone.
The murmuring tries to give her eyes
to decipher the words of abuse
into appeal, terror and loneliness,
into erased lips that long to rest

on the other´s erased palm. She reads.
And the wall shows the little boy with croup:
the blue light fluttering round his mouth.
And his mother running towards the neighbour´s farm
for twenty years, only a cry.

The sea breathes in the garden.
The children stand still and listen.
There´s a stubborn resistance in them.
In the space around them, in every direction,
the strict pattern of paradise stretches.
It expects obedience!
The children´s answers are calm questions.

Evening. The past awkwardly approaches
the translucent figures at the kitchen table
as if it wanted to clarify.
The girl checks herself in mid-sentence
her hand to her throat. Like the choked boy!
No thumping, no squeezing of her rib will help.
The trembling fingers can´t get down her throat.
The colour of the past flares in her face.
All distances suddenly enormous;
the very door already out of sight.
Not even the *word* "help" exists.
A despair greater than anyone in the room
lifts her up and down, shakes her like a clod.
And succeeds.

The clasped shuddering child
is breath after breath, breath after breath.
The kitchen is nothing but evening sun.
Panes of sun, table of sun,
skin of sun, low words of sun.

Their fragile hours of summer,
their slow breathings

lay a duty. The dead boy is still in the room
with his stiffening face.
The world is being lost.
The world must come into being.
Much is demanded of many.

The children compose themselves.
Listen to master sea.
Who is in everything invisibly.
Breathes through the white house in the dusk.
Breathes in the darkening trees
and the widely branching unease of the sleepers.
Breathes in pale space.

FAMILY GATHERING

This park with its over-bright floating tree-tops
and its drifting cow-parsley
round the semblance of an inn
is a chance meeting-place.
One comes here with a piece of oneself,
a fragment of anonymous suit,
a pinch of watchful courtesy
and warped memories of the family—
to test them against others´ misunderstanding
in the hope that the bits can be pieced into
a pattern beyond one´s own experience:
a family portrait disclosing the individual´s place.
And showing a stump of freedom´s boundary.

Now, they assemble here for a photograph,
an already over-exposed company.
The whitened children in different directions
at once. The dead, enticed out
by the rank scent of the questions,
are looking for their places
in those at present living. Also uninvited
kin jostle, interbred, irrelevant
to the day´s festivities but hard to turn away.
In the back row stands the narrator.
A farmer from the time of Charles the Fifteenth
tries to come into him, deceptively like
the Indian chief Geronimo, with deep-set
merciless eyes and a face of leather
in the sparse preacher´s beard. Is visible
when looked at. Of course, he tries to press his eye-balls
into the younger´s, to see through them
and give them his sight. The younger parries,
grasps the aged beard.

Wait. Here´s a yellowed photo
that sheds light on the situation:

grandfather and the boy at the grindstone.
The old man turns the handle,
his dwindling powers seek a way
through spindle and stone to the young heart.
The boy resists, less and less gets through
the thinning edge pressed against the stone.
Within the old man: an emptiness
crying for his favourite daughter Märit.
Was at her death that he "went Evangelical"
and made himself more and more like the prophets
who have nothing to repent. He is well-read
in *The Knowledgeable Schoolmaster*. His experience,
gleaming, half-transparent
like the outhouse window behind them,
he wants to transmit through this alien boy
too fine in his Sunday best. He'll write, that's sure,
let the old man see with cleansed eyes,
speak with young and steady voice.
There's so much knowledge to glean,
I'll show the lad how we read the tracks of God.
There's so much he wants in others.
But the edge pressed to the stone thins.
The emigrating soul is checked
by the steel's ever sharper resistance
and is scattered in sparks between them.

Such a resistance in the grouping, too.
The living brush off the thoughts of the dead,
a haze of flies that persists, persists.
Ready to click. Should be possible
to see the real family gathering here—
the gathering of the dead in each and all,
how they jostle and wrangle in each and all,
how they bargain, give and take,
and at last agree on an identity.

To grasp what's happening here
one must identify the dead. A general fervour.

Some push into the circle: Lasse from Espnäs
with two skins in the 1542 accounts.
An unexpected relation is Jens Joenssön,
the family renegade. Lost his farm at Öhn
for taking the Swedish oath in the Kalmar war.
And this is still further off-scene:
lichen for a beard and a gleam on his face
from the wash-house where his wife is screaming
alone with the flames: the door locked
by a strut—fallen? put there?
He was acquitted but the prosecutor demands
a retrial—after three centuries—
elbows forward through the crowd, embittered.
By mistake assails the solid farmer
who seized a burning log from the fire
when the wolves nuzzled at the door in 1815
and thrust it in the pack-leader´s teeth.
What was it he recognised?

Countryfolk from Skåne and a throng of strangers
mix with these hundreds from Jämtland.
This farmer, without the family features,
is the village artist
who painted his dream on wooden beaters and swingles.
The stone lion under his arm is clearly Assyrian
and shows how long his art has been on the way:
the legs are worn quite out.
His mother lingers in the background
among the heavily pruned willows.
Will only, half-averted through shyness,
let it be known that after all she slept with the Count
and that certain noses and talents
should be interpreted accordingly.
She is one of the few to have any colour:
ephemeral pastel, too much pink.

–What nonsense! She who protests

must have been born a grandmother.
Straddles as if she were very fat.
What in God's name is she holding the belt for?
Can a descendant's memory of a good hiding
distort the past that much? Is history so soft?
Just what she meant!
Here the serfdom of the dead is passed over.
They're there, in the daily toil:
it's from them that strength comes.
Yet they must stand where the view of the living insists.
And may be seen only in the twisted guise
a later person lends them.
But now they demand justice!

Justice? This man has something to do with her, it seems,
but what he holds out is a rope:–This is my justice.
No descendant will see that knot.
My death became...heart failure,
a decent fever. And the bottles
which were a name for my self-contempt,
these they have swept up.
Just as I tidied myself out of the world.

Catching his sick glance
as he tosses the rope over a branch.
One is expected to stare at the swinging loop
while he furtively slips round one
to pass his hands from behind
into one's own. Resistance!

But where should the resistance be applied?
These scattered notices about the dead
fall in with the wishes of the living
and have nothing further to tell
of the mafia's gathering in one. The real context,
the one focussed in this burning face,
remains inaccessible. The eye
leaves all these coaxed witnesses.

And so the pattern appears:
voices and steps from the meeting families
chrystalise in a shape which *should* be the narrator
but is the over-bright figure beside him,
so like it must be a twin,
only with another loyalty in his back,
most like a bureaucrat
with professionally open skull,
honest as wool, of course,
listening in to the centre of power, though.
But that other one does not exist.
The uncertainty of the system
has produced a half-metre miss
and an unexpected freedom.
The aged figures around are clearly disturbed
by this limit to participation.

Round the too-white coffee-table
under the trees' wandering tops
a world clamours: centuries and climates
throng in the park. The hand
that stirs in the quite immaterial cup
absently frees itself from a thousand hands.
Shining with their energy.
He who tells this shares the features of many
in the quarrelsome gathering.
And they demand their right in him!
But the movement in what he says
is another word for freedom.

THE ROYAL LIBRARY, OCTOBER 4TH

The reading room:
a piece of aged groping brain
obsessed by the past.
Meaningless fag-ends of gossip,
a flicker of faces and situations
here and there amid emptiness and gold leaf
between the pillars and the desks of researchers
where scattered ambitions sit hunched
like signalmen with scratching pens.

This iron door leads to the underground.
The pounding grows louder.
The winding iron stairway
leads down through boundless halls
level upon level, with pungent drifting smoke
and an indefinable rumbling. This is History:
quite unstructured, possible to grasp
only through the questions one brings from outside.
A vague impression of wooden bars, a little to one side.
Possibly shifting firelight, keys being turned in locks.
But nothing is in safe keeping.
Here is a vertiginous void
behind whole peoples vanished for ever.

"Lend me a little life." A voice quite close.
And space down here heels over.
Incomprehensible.

The steps down, the groping questions
are assumed to serve the common memory
that is constantly breaking up. Such great pains
to reconstitute the loud-voiced discourse
through time and space
where each word, each action, takes up a position.
But only here
will the individual voice be comprehensible.

The questions rouse a throng of the dead.
But they turn away.
Their backs are mere exasperation.
As if one were despatched by an imperial power
to extend its oppression over these figures of the past
instead of finally
giving *them* their justice.

But didn´t one hang up
most of one´s age´s identity
up there in the cloakroom?
And isn´t one now standing here
extending an almost peeled hand,
barely of the 1970s,
a hand that acquires no meaning
until someone down here grasps it?

The curt silence of the dead replies:
"What do *you* mean by meaning?
What questions do you put to your questions?"
There is something they see!

Yes—there is a powerful interference here.
Here, two steps in front of one,
a shape moves one can´t comprehend
for lack of experience.
Scattered thoughts, sparse absences,
tossed lumps of swelling dough,
move in a powerless searching.
The hands, perceptible as a lack of touch,
make their way among the oncomers:
"Lend me a little life, dammit!"
With accents of: scrape me away.
God, is he trying to pawn his liver?
Poking around in and beyond himself. Whatever
someone could in error
take as a thing of value.
Finds nothing.

Somewhere in nowhere
one still seems to have reached a price.
He waits, shaking.

Then an enormous needle pierces
his body,
that which one´s terror
makes to a body,
meets resistance first then wins through.
He seems to crave it himself
but it´s clear this girder of a needle
is directed from outside
by interests stronger than his.
Now he´s pinned like an insect, against nothing.
His legs run but can´t move him.
His eyes twist, to and fro,
to and fro
but find no light.
To and fro.
Stop, empty and dark.

But this is not history!
One staggers up the steps,
rushes through the reading room, it´s getting bigger and
    bigger:
an expanding Siberia.

From the front steps of the library—see the ambulance
and the stretcher they´re wheeling in
with a curled embryo shape
in an experienced Icelandic pullover.
A hand´s breadth of back bare, quite defenceless.
He´s been dead for a few seconds.
The syringe rolls to and fro in the basin
in the still lurching toilet in the cellar.
A few metres from the scholarly questions.

THE CATHEDRAL IN CHARTRES

Coming here in great confusion.
Not even a memory that could prompt.
As if something I´d lost had taken it too,
something I should have kept
in the throng of indifference.
The world: clouds in transit, torn fields.
Labyrinthine roads all leading
to death. The circling buzzard, the red sun—
are all vital signs. But incomprehensible.

Here they have raised a coherence,
a doctrinal system of soaring stone
in the midst of chaos. They´re pulling down
the mortar-stained props under the vaults
and existence quietens in clear lines
and morning-cool space, held fast
by strict rays of light
and the first notes of a kyrie
without end. Here the world is real
for him who says yes. Outside:
no values that stay. No road will obey a map.
Step into the pattern.

The canon preaches: this is incarnation´s
ground. And rags of souls find their way here
from all of earth´s perplexed corners—
to become flesh and obedience,
a common body without all private faces
which are only question by question. And this flesh
is still Word, quite without fleshliness.

What a supreme temptation.
Swallows flit, distinctly, along the roof,
a faith substantiated
without a feather, without a single dropping.

Stand, myself, in an indeterminate muddy street:
a gaze that probes the unfaltering flying-
buttresses, a heart whose beat now and then
falters, steps that know how the ground gives way
and how reality each hour must be defined anew.

In here in the half-lit gloom:
so many guilt-oppressed backs
have fitted themselves into the nave floor
and been transformed to rugged participation,
so many willingly split open breasts
in the weightless pointed arches—
a view opened for all,
so many who renounced name and bewilderment
to enter an authority
that raises its firmament arch by arch.
He who inserted himself as a key-stone,
a head-rest for an arch,
is now one single petrified rapture.

Here art too is obedience.
The master who fitted piece to piece
of his imperfect glass
uses its bubbles and scratches to force
the light into a perfect language.
And loses himself in the greater syntax.
His apprentices stand there gaping
with their glass left-overs.

The stranger pauses before a work
the believers hurry past, the Butcher´s Window:
protected by the prophet Ezekiel
who raises his right hand and averts his glance,
a local butcher stands,
pieced together by glass, his axe raised
over a tethered resistance. Can´t imagine
the cathedral without *that* window!

In this building, it´s said,
twenty cathedrals are on the way.
The building-master strikes his plan: This is Europe!
We have to contradict him.

In the furthest shadow from the north tower
this rose-garden, a blossoming persistence. Somewhere,
notes from a kind of stringed instrument
with a warmth felt down the groin.
Whoever is absent-mindedly plucking the strings
is thinking with his senses.
Such a sweet confusion. The unknown intelligence,
shaping notes with the fingers, has still no alternative
but feels its way, for now,
forward to a NO.

ESCORIAL

This building is intangible
although its weight makes the earth groan.
Has the shape of St. Lawrence's grill.
Neither castle nor cloister but both at once,
a building of rough suspiciousness.
Its lead roof a shield against heaven's gaze.

The windows of power are small.
Standing inside one of them now,
by a shimmer of landscape in bubbled glass,
possibly leaded. A hint of tile
with blue pruned leaves rings me in.
Have acquired a crumb of identity. Where from?
Here, it seems, that entails risk.
Questions and answers. My curiosity
gives to the abstract the guise of a room.
And *that* tries to give me a name.
Would like...the impulse is absorbed at once.
Sense another will in the room, sinewy
thoughts stretching away over the heights.
The rain streaming aslant over the slope
veers. In here there's a wandering ache
that rises from the study table
—it exists, then—
throws itself on the bed—it exists—
sleepless in the alcove, rests on elbows
by the little window giving on the high altar
where the madonna's lips are still moving.
Her eyes frightened, turned steadily this way
towards the will that rises in disgust:
I, Philip, by the Grace of God—

As if these rough blocks of granite
were sucking in my brain-cells:
the king needs the help of others

to raise the palace round himself.
But if this is an exchange of thoughts—
what do *I* get from power?
The flow must be made visible.

Now only one is permitted to speak:
From this chamber at the mountain's foot
I rule the old world and the new
with two inches of paper—
Scarcely distinguishable.
If only power would make itself clear.

Here perhaps. The library shows its temptation
among books with spines in and gold out:
the cosmic globe with the courses of the stars,
borne by four women with lions' feet.
Empty intangible spheres
circling and soughing through each other.
There is the soundless roaring Lion,
there the timeless stinging Scorpion.
The prince stands musing before these strict
heavenly arcs that decide the fates of all.
Hear the faint swish through the globe,
the swish of a higher will
free from every human bent.
The ever stronger pain through the body:
this rot that more and more becomes *him*.
The stiff hand slowly reaches
in among the globe's arcs.
Overcomes its trembling.
And the fingers make the course of the stars
conform to the will *here* in this room:
Men hesitate out on the fields
facing their new lives. At the crossroads
the carter reins in the rearing horse
and chooses another direction; the first
scraped out of his head.

The past has been replaced. The lovers
no longer recognise each other.
It is clear now: power chooses its people.

A strange charge in the air in here.
The pages of the opened book stand on end.
And the down on the back of my hand has risen.
A smell of conspiracy—
Lightning and thunder simultaneous.
The basilica´s struck! Is the Tempter´s laughter
rolling down through the valley. Echoes, echoes:
thunderstrokes and laughter from all sides.
In the dazzled eye there remains
the picture the lightning showed:
another Spain within his Spain,
low countries in perpetual revolt.
The one clarity has given the other.

The hand that altered the stars in their courses
is for a moment powerless. But clenches:
Guard out! Send for the Grand Inquisitor.
All roofs shall be lifted off houses.
All souls shall be scrubbed.
Look into every testicle. List
every thought that touches upon power.
And the soldiers worry along alleys and opinions.
The pyres flare, away through the centuries.

Our talk didn´t give the king much of a face,
only a bloodshot suspiciousness
to see with, a grizzled drooping moustache
to sniff enemies with.
Who did *you* become?
Groping over sudden features
with trembling fingertips—
I clearly have some distinctive lines
suspected of having to do with resistance

in the low countries. And Europe?
What became the sign of Europe? Fumble
in despair. A single earthy letter would do!
No. That word belongs to power, still.
Quite abstract.

But the resistance is there. And it's Philip himself
who specifies his enemies. It's him
who gives their weapons substance,
yes, presses muskets into the hands
of those who refuse to touch a weapon.
His soldiers rove, stab at random
a coming year, a thinkable thought.
The king himself stands in aged dread
before all those drafts of faces,
this rage at rage
his very glance creates.

THE TIME OF THE GREAT WAR

You—walking the grass above me
as if you looked for a land
not there yet
are you trying to see my attempt to think?
Only if you ask for me
have I something to say to you
since all that was I was struck out.
I am only a claim
that doesn´t relinquish. That I am gone
has nothing to do with death and corruption.
I am more definitely gone.
The very day I stood at the edge
of the deep trench we dug,
the very woods around us,
the light trembling down through the needles
have been scraped out of history.
I see it clearly, detail by detail,
exactly as it´s missing. As if you´d asked me.
But all replaced by a foreign text.
My death has never taken place.

Despite that, my life persists.
It´s not much. An itching darkness against the eyes.
An upward wrenching pain over the back.
That´s all. I try to interpret it.
The only possibility is a greatcoat
pulled up over the head
and fastened with a loop round the neck,
the arms tied behind and twisted up
and connected to the loop so
that each attempt to lower them
will tighten it round the throat.
Technically, it might fit,
if such is possible to men.
I remember nothing of the world

but have a notion
that much is possible to men.

At times I try to fabricate a memory.
Always the same scene.
A small, very bright room
with an incomplete cross on the wall.
People sitting at the table,
a woman, two or three children.
The picture has so much to do with me
that for a moment I have a breath
to lose.
They have no faces.
As if someone had taken their faces.
One chair is empty. There´s a force in the picture
wanting to take away that empty chair as well
as if it said too much
but my thoughts resist.
I´m fighting with someone over the picture!
If one looks closely one can see the scruff
left by the knife that scraped between the figures
by the empty chair
and the sheen from the pencil
which clumsily filled the space
with a carved chairback
and the same leaves as on the wallpaper behind
but hesitated at the missing piece
of the cross. The woman and children round the table
have been deprived of more than their identity.
In what´s left of their foreheads there are signs
of scraping *under* the bone as well.
They can´t even forget
him who is not at the table.
There´s no longer anyone to forget.
They sit quietly round the steaming soup
without touching it, lost
in a sorrow without contents.

All this is in the cloth
itching against the eye-sockets.
There are words to say to them,
those three, maybe four, at the table
but dissolved in the lime in mouth and senses.

Let me borrow your voice.

The lime has also blotted out
name and trace of the executioners.
They must have had a language.
There must have been commands that drove
us prisoners forward to the edge.
The stabs were there. They will witness to
the square bayonets, their again and again.
And the bullets. With remnants of expertise
coming from I don´t know where
I know the calibre: 7.65. Feel
that´s contradictory evidence.
But what I´m fumbling for
is not to expose the executioners.
They´ll be brooding under their own grass.
It´s something else I want to prove.
What my attempt at thinking speaks against,
crawling forward through the lime,
is this white page where the woods should be,
these empty lines
instead of the stinking execution-site,
this scraped site in history
where we belong.
The torment twisting under the skull
is that nothing of this took place.

If Europe some day
somewhere is to exist
part of it must be called
respect for what took place.

BÉLA BARTÓK AGAINST THE THIRD REICH

Haven´t you any ration-cards?
Here in France people are starving.
You need two coupons to breathe,
three to see. He knows, at home everywhere
on this meaningless continent.
Each street a lonely line on the hand.

Must look him up here in Nîmes,
at the moment he´s to leave Europe.
At the breaking-point.

An interview without questions and answers.
His table is only two metres away
but the distance is unconquerable.
He is a silence of 49 kilos
with a flame instead of a glance.
Lays aside knife and fork
on the little fish-skeleton
and raises his last drop of Perrier to...
Checks himself.

At the corner an imaginary Citroën
watches, two men in drawn-down hats:
a part of the meaningless.
They´ll split this October evening in Provence
between words and coolness.
Everything they touch becomes abstract. Him here
a number. Comment: voluntary non-Arian;
his letter to Goebbels
demanding that he too
be counted among the *entartete Musiker*
is signed by a Jew.

But can a few bars in a string-quartet
obstruct a tank?

The spies' unease betrays: they're not quite sure.

What matters now are the signals to him
from a village in northern Slovakia:
continuous screeching and whistling.
And he who has the code receives it, tense.
Hasn't even set his glass down. His hearing—
an amazing amplifier—takes in each leaf
falling on the distant square.
Crackling voices crowd round his table.
To the men in the car
the distant sorrow pouring in
is divided into signs and gnashing of teeth,
incomprehensible but manageable.

He is shaken by a brittle rage:
They are non-humans, their language is separation.
They keep the human in man
apart from what they call man.
They keep the acrid smoke
away from the word "measure."
That makes everything possible.

So long as one street in Hungary has the Beast's name
no plaque will be set up in my memory,
no market-square will take my name.

The square. The signals frantic. Come
from clay and sky, a life without roads,
with perpetually foreign conquerors, these
are inside the village chapel:
they've dragged the hostages there. The congregation split
between the impalpable pain inside
and the silent cries out in the square.
Assembly forbidden. None of the desperate
may exist for another.
They've been split into abstract fellowship
and scattered fragments of introvert song,

hunched shoulders that sing.

So well he knows them. For decades has had
each voice, each note on a wax roll:
traces depicting fraternization
right through sparkling barbed wire—
rhythms that begin in distant rythms,
villages that continue in remote villages.
These isolated voices, voice beyond voice,
know what´s being dragged out in the square:
something no longer perceptible.
And now they seek him out.
An opening in rasping quarter-tones
to a limitless score.

I must leave Europe.
The only way I can articulate *Europe*.

It´s getting late here in Nîmes.
The evening is split between the word "evening"
and an incomprehensible falling darkness.
Only those who leave
can come here.
He is on the way.
But the meaningless have touched him
with their non-hands. He is split
between abstract despair that travels
and harsh music that stays behind, unwritten.
Years can pass before it reaches him.

He is on the way
and not on the way, yet.

A BOOK TO BURN

You´re leafing through my experiences,
these pages I should have burnt.
Yet see nothing. Don´t you understand?
You´re looking for some line to quote
from the old master Li Zhi. And that
is fruitless. Nobody puts his finger
on my words. I wrote as the hare jumps
and the falcon strikes. Not to agree with the reader,
nor to pencil in the kind of quote
you call a masterpiece.
I wrote in the margins of others´ books,
questioning between the lines,
and refuting when a blank left room.
So don´t agree. Doubt my words
and see *your* role in the writing made clear—
but only quickly to slip out
of the new snare which knows who you are.
And the falcon takes to the air again.

I myself lived in a larger text
among illegible public officials
in a mumbling about the Emperor´s duties to Heaven
while they created behind his back
the strong Style
without a single separate voice.
I was born to break up that text.
A chance occurred in the year of the Boar.
But my words, so trained to strike,
hesitated. So many excuses.
My agility dwelt in the brush of the scribe.
I sludged along like army-worms,
never alone, no, a clan on two legs,
one head with thirty mouths to feed.
Thirty souls heading for one office—
how could I wriggle out of that hunger?

And revolt provides only a new syntax,
the heroes always the same.
On the utmost tip of a hair
they found another monastery.

Thus excuses gathered before my house
and the moment passed.
Too late I grasped my real motive.
I hoped to change the importance of the moment
for the eternity of my marginal notes.
And was doomed to see my prayers granted.
I wrapped my achievement in a grain of dust
and I come like the iron-shod wheel of the Law.

This scrawl in the margins of others' thoughts
has been collected and called *A Book to Burn*.
I believed that those I'd exposed
would seek my life. Now I know
that words are riskier than that
and that fire seeks them through the centuries.
The real signs
burn already in the brush-stroke.
The good thought tastes of smoke.

How I miss you, my friends, prepared
to refute all that I wrote, suffering
the same impatience, the same anger as myself.

Instead of you I get eternity:
one of the false, affirmative signs.
Yes, I wanted it! But within my want
I wanted to undo all conclusions.
When my colleagues kept on about the Only Thing
I interrupted them, advising them
to devote their day to the joys of begetting
and then go out with their women in the moonlight,
listening to a solitary lute

and feeling the air cool their necks.
No wonder
I was considered dangerous to the State
and thrown into prison. At last
with the razor as my only friend.

Still I want to conclude one thing:
when your moment in history comes—
don´t look for excuses,
they will certainly queue on your stairs.
Enter the words awaiting you
with smouldering edges.
Or take over my death.
I shall throw it across your fleeing back
like the corpse of a dog.

I'M STILL CALLED OSIP MANDELSTAM

No, this is not migraine.
It's the remains of an assignment
beating
still in the emptiness.

I just find it so hard to breathe, Nadia.
As if we lay in our bunks
staring at the roof: a throng so dense
it finds no place in the word "throng."
This barracks is a mass grave
where we share each other's death. Hear the others'
slow thoughts groping in the room
for a window. Just as clearly
as the smell of urine here.

At last I learned,
dissolved in fever and excrement,
to think with the body.
And the current passing through the room
(where from?) gives me strength.
Someone is breathing for me.

Manage to think I raise myself on one
arm and stare through the window.
Nothing seems to have been changed:
the empty landscape, the lack of oxygen,
the Siberian smell of loneliness—all
the same. Our Land's Father knew to an inch
how death's kingdom is composed. Already lived
as if the land didn't exist.
His eyes just a stiff paranoia to see with,
the moustache just a wolf-grey wrath that scented
another Russia in the middle of his Russia,
a land that makes the land visible.
But the stars low, pliable images
that gave the signals he required.

How those who administer reality
fear poetry: an unexpected resistance
making it possible to see.

They had quite simply to choke my voice.
Snipped me out of readers´ memories
the way one cuts a page from the Encyclopedia.
For he whom no-one listens to
is choked by his own words.
Now five deep breaths tell me
you saved my manuscripts
and some read what I wrote. Someone
turns a page: gives me words to see with.
See the empty window-frame. The pail
in the corner: a dented stink of ideology.
I see quite clearly that I´m dead.
I see that changes nothing.
New words make their way from the mouth
and move through the emptiness here.
They´ll find me lousy with poetry
although the room was fumigated.

No-one writes after their death, you say.
But that´s wrong, Nadia.
If I stopped
your heart would stop beating
and Russia remain a desolate idea.

You don´t dare believe?
I see your doubt branching
outside the window, a hinted green.
My word settles swaying down in it,
a few trial notes, an arabesque
forcing the indeterminate green to leaves,
each one precise, with five fingers.
For one minute perhaps the word turns
this non-existent tree
into a maple

and the tree turns the word into a goldfinch
swaying in the branch-tip. No note
is where it could be expected.

The road is for a minute clear—
but it´s the road from Vladivostok.
And you are standing on it.
Feel you standing staring in my darkness.
Don´t stop breathing for me!
I raise my hand in your breeze.
The muddy plain holds a Mediterranean.
The fins of dolphins deep under the earth
plough without pause, like the writer´s hand.
A Crete with heights of gleaming skin
is caught in the clay. The waves rise,
scarcely able to hold back their "Yes"—

Darkness. It´s much too soon.
My lonely thought is cold.
How did the concept "cloak" come into my hands?
Must be you who sent it.
So worn it is. I´ve nothing to mend it with.
But it is a cloak all right.
I quickly wrap it round the shivering land.

Must have more patience.
Must begin with what´s near.

Now I shall think of a humble word:
earwig. Scampers on the window-sill
no, where one could expect a window-sill,
pedantically precise
but impossible to foresee. Seems
to move unscathed out and in of death,
out of my world, into yours.
Now it short-cuts across a finger.
Which for a moment exists. The word´s
resistance is a sudden joy.

THE IMPERIAL ARMY IN XÍAN

What kind of consuming light is it
we´re stumbling towards? Unarmed.
My sword is only a void in my grasp.
The wooden handle mouldered
and the bronze fallen to the ground, verdigrised
and brittle as egg-shell. Feel
the others´ appalled faces in my own.
My twitching muscles grope in theirs,
don´t reach our ecstasy,
the rigid screams above the lips,
the vertigo that made us implacable.
Here in the vanguard not one coat of mail—
in our meeting with the future
our armour was to be intoxication,
for which we wait, trembling, a crowd
of fragments leaning into each other, shamefully
taking support in others. Understand nothing:
thought our army was invincible.

A little to the side
I sense the hind-quarters of a horse:
merely a stiffened neighing from the earth.

I am half-way still in sleep.
Only a moment ago
I owned senses. Was sought by someone
as close as my own skin, kneeling,
a strand of hair tensed by the comb,
falling to the ground
when the lips seek my beating groin
and still defend their conduct
through the centuries I´ve been away:
a face increasingly dissolved,
a voice increasingly evaporated,
the only one who knew my loneliness.

Nothing now exists except this light.
Nothing else has ever taken place.

An archer, close by, kneeling
with bow tensed towards the throbbing light,
without wood, without string, and the arrow-head,
corroded, fallen to the ground.
He must have had a name. Or was
there not a name to be forgotten?
Yet I gather from the context
he is our best archer:
his mouldered arrow never misses its mark.
But what is his mark?
He has only terror where his gaze should be.
His lips are tight from what he sees.
Tightening black earthenware lips.
There's a handsbreadth of skin on his back,
quite defenceless, it bubbles and blackens,
a flaking text, for no-one.
This is an ultimate loneliness.

A loneliness in 38 formations.

I rush forwards, my hat
a bird rising from my head.
We stagger in collapsing order
into the growing light.
With an aching flake of brick for an eye
I see the flickering is full of shapes
flaring white.
They come towards us with intoxicated faces,
merciless. I recognise them!
Recognise the features as our own.

I have one thought left,
more a coiling emptiness behind
my brow and hard to keep hold of.

But I sense that you whose hopes are on us
should have known our helplessness.
The bird that lifted from my head
from these dispersing shards
brings you tidings of our helplessness.

THE FIRST SHADOW IN THE WALL

What is it you demand of me?
I don´t remember anything
and don´t even know the purpose of your meeting.
I´m only a darkness on the brick surface,
possibly with a human outline.
But as I live on the surface
I have no past.
My thought circles
between the small blackness in the brick
the one that is me
and the enormous sky in the wall
the one that is nothing but sun.
If the circling reached out by a fingerbreadth
my thought could climb as in a spiral staircase,
look down and think it understands
one floor more than before.

I sometimes dream of space
and wake up dizzy.
The part of the brick surface which is my breast
can sometimes almost feel a hand,
my lips in the mortar joint
almost perceive a probing finger,
throbbing in three dimensions,
the recesses of a fingerprint.
Such a vertiginous roughness.

But the fingers running over me
belong to a group of visitors, a preposterous world
where you can lean towards me
without being in me
and read at a shameless distance
with your fingers in my pelvis.
They fumble over the black text
as if suspecting it´s about them.
Only burning fingers would understand.

Leave me alone.
Let me walk in the sparse grass.
Yes, I´m arrested
among very distinct shadows of grass.
Far away the shadow of a tree
with a few stray leaves. I think
I´m on my way to someone.
I think I´m a woman.
But I don´t know if I´m young or old.
That thought can´t be carried out.

There´s no change here
but moments of insight.
Then I can feel
that the loneliness is shared by many, many
in a realm that grows
without therefore getting larger.
We reach each other with our fingertips.
No one can put his hand in another´s
since nothing can lift from the surface.
No one can move on top of another
in a shadow of lust.
But we barely touch each other and shudder
in the dark light that fills the surface.

Here are no clouds, no birds.
Shadows of dogs but no barking.
It´s autumn or spring. Rain
is one of unthinkable things.
Like muddy wheel tracks. Houses
are absurd, of course. Gangs are prowling the streets
to plunder the very word "house."
Still there´s a kind of order here.
The last are indeed the last.
Instead of mentioning them
we hold four fingers in the air.

What do you want me to tell you?
Here are doors but no rooms.
Here are voices but no echo.
Everything is shortened as if history
had taken a short cut right through me.
So when you call me out of my stone
to witness
you demand an absurdity.
Here is no "out of."

Call the empty place among you
mine. I must stay where I stand.
It's the only way I can speak to you.

Hiroshima

OUTSIDE THE CALENDAR

from *När vägen vänder/Route Tournante*
(1992)

from *Det andra livet/The Other Life*
(1998)

from *De levande har inga gravar/The Living Have
No Graves*
(2002)

WHEN A LANGUAGE DIES

When a language dies
the dead die a second time.
The sharp word that turned the earth
in damp glistening furrows,
the chipped word with steaming coffee,
the bright and slightly flaked word
that for a moment reflected
the window and the noisy elm outside,
the secret sweet-smelling word
the hand sought in the dark
with shy assurances:
these words which gave the dead a life
beyond life
and the living a share in a greater memory
have just been scraped out of history.

So many shadows scattered!
Without a name to live in
they are forced into final exile.

The sign on the overgrown station
is called something with 54 letters
which no-one can get their mouth round any more.
That we could put up with. If only all those
who died for the second time
had not taken the roughness of earth away with them,
the green of the foliage, the coolness from the stream.
The foot can suddenly go right through the ground.
And no-one knows what the wind wants with us
or why we once came here.
Of course we can hear the birds in the tree
but what has become of the song?

HOW WRONG, YET HOW PERSISTENT...

How wrong, yet how persistent—
that Eurydice with a fading cry
would return to depths and darkness!
She recoiled—yes—from his terrified stare
for who´d want to be seen eight days after death?
Unwillingly, though, she did follow
that familiar stranger
who sang her out of facelessness
day after day after day
and overwhelmed her protests.
She lived long by his side
without living by his side.
Hard to understand
how she could drink a goblet of wine
without drinking a drop
or how she could walk in the sun
with steps groping in the dark.
Only the man she thought she loved
and reached for with hesitant finger-tips
seemed now and then to understand
when he embraced longing and air.

SUNDAY AT MUSEO FRIDA KAHLO

After all that happened the house is closed:
a tattered communist dream
is restored in there, supervised
by the ex-lodger Trotsky.

We´ve obtained permission to visit
but meet a distrustful wooden eye
in the hole of the green street-door:
"But you have just been in here."

We must wait while the guard seeks advice
from higher powers. A humming-bird waits with us,
a searching flutter at rest: like time
it sucks honey from the stone itself.
Above the wall the world ash-tree towers.

At last we are granted a repeat.
There are signs we´ve been here before
though none of us can remember—
tracks of my heels in the sand,
our whitened names in a guest book of wood.
And Papa Kahlo, the photographer in his frame,
regards us with completed face;
his camera contains, for several hours now,
my turned-away side
which only his sensitive film can see.

Here are Frida´s crutches and iron corset.
And the child´s corpse beside its broken up mother.
What scrupulous accounts we audit:
paint tubes, nails, ecstasies and tips.
She has learned from The Implacable Bookkeeper,
Stalin, prop of steel for a wounded world.
Then doesn´t she see: his giant head, averted,
looking askance at her little one,

has rationed even its smiles!
His hand is strangling the flying bird.

But here are the two Fridas.
(The one seeking her secret sister
must find the milk-shop
opening towards the inside of earth.)
An artery runs from the one heart
into the other:
the two have a common blood circulation.
What could Diego hope for?

"You, my dear, who are born every hour,
only I can give what you already have."
"I know. And only I can have from you
what you never had."

It is one and the same heart
but two troubled faces.
The one was here a minute ago,
the other has just arrived.
(And the one who seeks her turned-away half
must find the trivial door.)

Trotsky drags back the two chairs
he nicked when he moved.
Not that the squalor troubles him.
But history must be retouched
to let the Dream come true.

The last is not the popular skeletons,
caught in a kind of mazurka.
The last is the turtle
slowly swimming through centuries
and yet remaining in this room.
Has started to crumble from all it has seen.

PRAGUE QUARTET

1.
So many listening. Seeming to recognise.
Like the castle on its hill—a scoured head
filled with suspicions, shelf upon shelf.
It's 1985 and will remain so.
The houses up there are hanging on
although they've long since lost their foundations.
Only the cathedral has weight and time,
half of it gusts of wind, half of it stone:
an old man with a stroke
fumbling for words to express his rage.

A devastation is at work here
which the senses can barely grasp
yet they find it surprisingly familiar.
As if thrashing wing-beats
and tearing claws... No, the austere space
contradicts our presentiments:
"No more's happening here than Liberation!"

One piece of the past, at least, left:
John of Nepomuk being tumbled into the river
by hands which have failed to loosen his tongue.
As if frozen in a fall from a police office window.
Buttercups and carnations are heaped before his place
with an old-fashioned appeal:
"Free us from denunciation!"

Wing-beats and claws... It sounds
like a culture vanishing.
The scent of lilac is suddenly a phrase
and one more instalment inaccessible.

This street was once a piece of Europe.
So many languages, so many ways of thinking

and room for them in an ale-house
the size of an open hand.
The singing from the open window
wants listeners to recognise—
What do we mean by "recognise?"

Those small remnants of flesh
constantly whirling out of nothing—
the air glossy as if full of black beaks.
The people crossing the bridge—how they thin out!

We move in towards the old square.
The walls scraped, dull parchment
fighting against its new text.
Instead of faces, scratches and hacks.
The crowd on the square stiffens: a gnashing of thoughts.
As if something tried to be understood.

2.
The lovers are liberated slowly
from the suffocating evening.
The hotel room dissolving away.
Like the Ascension on the ceiling of St. Nicholas´:
they rise through the red smoke
in a stiffening whirl of sheets.
Legs hesitate a moment
dangling helplessly from the ecstasy
with magnified soles
before the azure absorbs them too.
Only the tottering houses are left,
arched into the sudden vacancy.

It´s quiet. Gradually
shy faces in the plaster
emanate round the waking onlookers:
with sprawling fingers St. Nicholas blesses
the money-changers in nervous jeans,

the double-bass master who lost his position
when he married in church,
the waitress struggling with the country's future—
a trayful of unwashable china.
Flaking faces, unexpectedly as close
as their own laboured breathing.

3.
Here Kafka is a poltergeist.
Exorcized from the book-shops
he now haunts each street in Prague
(which then becomes a street in Prague).
It's told how the minister M one night
met himself on Charles Bridge.
He's still being treated for what he learnt.
And a bus-load of Party-members from Bratislava
on a hungry visit to government headquarters
vanished with an unknown guide. At times
they can be heard inside the walls.
Is that him with a vague smile
hanging a warning-sign by Laterna Magika?
(The street beneath the entrance is gone.)
I spell my way through the foreign text
and see how the theatre audience insists,
floating in over the shaft's nerves and veins,
Prague's opened rib-cage:
they leaf through a coming year,
discuss its protagonists.
As if a new production were inescapable
in the inescapably closed theatre.

4.
The public spring condenses
in today's concert in St. Nicholas'.
Such lavish orthodoxy! Trumpets.
The choir steadily dissolving
heralds the People's liberation

from the people. And hold back 1985.
Trombones. Up on the plinth
power in a golden mitre incidentally
named St. Cyril of Alexandria.
Presses down his crozier on the throat
of the heretic, here called Nestorian.
The poor victim is bent backwards, bald with pain,
with holes instead of pupils.
Only the half-open mouth is alive—
his cry checked an inch before the stone.
But why these enormous ears?
Do we attribute to a choked dissident
such powers of hearing?

Fortissimo: the roof opens slowly
to the tornado of faith: the red haze
takes up it own into its kingdom.

Only a frightened scrap of sun
has reservations up in the galley,
hovers by the organ which Mozart played.
That glimpse is enough! Clarifies
what the heretic´s ears are waiting for:
a Beethovenian *Waldhorn*
in some corridor of the future. Hesitatingly
like a waking drunk clearing his throat.

Dreams! Czeslaw Miłos has just announced
that the order of Europe is as stable
as it was after the Vienna Congress.
But power is contemplating with its mitre off
preparing itself, just to be sure,
in case it is time for a quick change of clothes.

Ahead, perhaps a century away,
a freedom can be sensed so unbound
that anyone walking over Charles Bridge risks
being scattered with his own breath.

Then the demons will be driven from every house.
So long as excessive zeal doesn´t force
the bookshop out of the word "bookshop"
and the bridges out of the gloss "bridge."
The crozier will undoubtedly be broken that day
and the bald heretic will be free to speak.
But will the words succeed in leaving his mouth
any more than now, if there is no-one
concerned enough to listen
and scratched enough to recognise?

Questions. Questions.
It´ll certainly be a hundred years
before we see liberation from Liberation.

from JOTTED ON HISTORY'S MARGIN

6.
As if I were trying in vain to break free
of the faceless muttering darkness
pouring down the stairway,
landing by landing, century by century,
a darkness we know all too well.

In the hall outside the copper doors
all the thoughts ever thought have piled up.
What a condensed odour of dust in the gloom!

In the centre, the sarcophagi.
Like those of the Ming Dynasty
but smaller and more faded.
My skin starts twitching by the third one:
I sense it must be my own waiting grave.
But the guide, who has read my associations,
shakes his head and explains
in a voice hoarse with history
that this is the grave I've just stepped out of.

7.
This is one of history's ambushes.
For several hours or days
Leningrad has taken back its name.
And the policeman is leafing through my pocket-diary,
going through my memory line by line.
"May I explain, off the record..."
"There is no *off the record* here!"
The hand sweeps towards the Neva, the famished warehouses
the floating palaces, the uniforms
shivering in queues at the ferry.
He is sitting inside the answer.
But turns pages: suspects I have copied down
that line in Marx that cancels Marx.

I look at his hands,
the lead ring, and recognize
the Mesopotamian temple-ministrant
whose face kept the kingdom intact.

FOUR GREEK VOICES
FROM UNDER THE GROUND

1.
I am the most lonely of shadows.
The others avoid me
like the stench of an unhealing sore.
They won´t even let me carry a name
for fear of contagion. You think you know
I am the one who showed history the way
and let the Persians attack us from behind
at the pass in whatever it is called.
The others down here won´t even soil their thoughts
through acqaintance with my deceit. No-one
will admit I served Necessity,
that god who forces events
towards an end hidden from us
and demands we turn a deaf ear
when the skulls crumble like shells.
I wanted in a word to serve something greater
than human loneliness.

2.
Death was said to be glorious when bravely
                        you fall at the fore.
There was nothing glorious
to the man already on his knees
in the slash from behind on the shoulder-blade
or in the stab in the crotch.
Nothing glorious either about the women
who came by night
and snatched from me the fumbled picture
of the woman I never stopped loving
but search for in vain down here
without the picture to help my memory.
Have I been straying for one year or a thousand?
One thing I do know: I´m tireless in my search

for whoever wrote about that glorious death.
I´ve saved this little knife,
a rarity down here,
to slit the tongue out of his mouth.

3.
Do you know it is your misunderstanding
that plagues us dead most of all?
I´m a simple statue, the flat sort,
a woman with crossed arms
and a face scarcely begun,
but I´m not on that account without feelings.
To me it´s torture when you late barbarians
who have exhibited my nakedness
maintain I served fertility
or showed the way to the final kingdom.
No, I was put in the loved one´s grave
by the woman who didn´t dare follow him
yet wouldn´t abandon him to loneliness.
I was the one to get kisses of mud
and caresses of naked bone
intended for a living being.
Only a heart of stone could bear that.

4.
Not even the *name* Porphyry should have survived.
That I am still now and then glimpsed among you
is due to the diligence of my enemies.
Just come a little closer.
It´s not that my voice is timid
but it has been forced to take such diversions
that the words are as worn as old sandals.
My writings of my own cause have been burnt
by those who had a better point of view
and my thoughts taken away to be broken on the wheel
by my pious opponents.
What rescued me for the future

is their need to contradict me—
I reach you through their criticism.
If they had drowned me in the silence of the well,
tossed my books to the pigs
and given no hint of my opinions
then no cunning could have helped me this far.
It´s their zeal to silence me
which lets you hear my voice.
But don´t expect to see my face.
Whoever has to find his way
out of overwhelming argument
and grinding mockery
can´t lay claim to much substance.
You will have to make do
with half a smile here,
an over-experienced wrinkle there.
But between "neither" and "nor"
you will still sense my breathing.

IMPROMPTU

It is a battered day.
We have quarrelled,
blackening the plastered walls,
but found a way back
to you, to me.
I rise a little so my sweaty skin
leaves your skin with a rustle,
and settle my heart in yours,
one clay plate turned into another.

The window is open: May is blue.
In the beam above us death advances
a thousandth of an inch, with a tick.
But the rosefinch on its bare branch
sings, sings.
The down on his breast stirs in the wind.
How much greater the song
than the shaking body.

OUTSIDE THE CALENDAR

Sian Ka´an is Mayan
for the place where heaven is born.
Now the vault is a few hours old
but already larger than I´ve seen it:
a blue that´s used for the first time.

The boat is poled closer to the isle.
What is it that slows down my watch
and turns the dollar in my pocket into waste paper?
They are there! What archaic clapper-bills.
Half foliage,
the flock of spoonbill broods
on the days we fear and at the same time
hope for with our turned-away halves.

Now one of their flock descends
out of the blue depths,
legs outstretched towards the nest,
its huge pink wings flapping
and your heart slows down.
The bird sinks and sinks
with outspread plumage stilled.
It sinks and sinks.
Your tongue a rusk in your mouth.
I realize this is the point
where time can no more be conceived.

from ILLUMINATIONS

2.
The children are sitting beside each other
curiously white
in a white room at a white piano.
It is, yet is not our dining-room.
Their hair is so white the eye recoils.
They laugh when bottom line and top line
unexpectedly concur.
The music too seems white.
The children must be fifteen and twelve.
Hard to decide
since they weigh nothing
and the picture denies us a context.
But there´s something wrong with the light.
It is much too intense
also for these high windows.
Then we can see how the white wallpaper
darkens at edges, curls
and lets through a flame, then one more, and one more.

ROUTE TOURNANTE

Cézanne has set up a sullen easel
in what does not yet exist.
He is so well-versed in the geology
of absence, layer by layer, that already
the nakedness of canvas is wholly authentic.

The road that turns in last year´s grass
is still only a curve in the mind,
pilfered from an old Chinaman.
It originates in a grimy chapter
he has scraped away with his knife—
you were never there!

Begin with the shadows
and work in towards the brightening centre.
The blue-grey can entice a field back.

Like his life this treacherous year:
the throbbing foot that won´t heal
and could consider leaving him.
While the road that wills, once more—
what thirst for the sun.

Among the women in dark head-scarves
his mother walks stooped in the dead man´s grief.
When the others have vanished round a bend
she makes excuses
to hang on like a blue haze above the road.

So hard to bear other touching—

It´s colour that can touch the world.
Of course he has mentioned logic. And the cone.
But these are approximate values.
No theory can get hold of

the furious energy inside things.
Only a grasp of colours
can force "reality" to a response.

Dab by dab, a dogged colour-scale
lifting a village out of the village:
gables, a steeple, a possible road
and a fugue of swallows.
Each house is uninhabited: is waiting
for whoever can summon strength to return.
A day is a year.

Like his life—
took decades to see that verdure is blue.
And now in a moment or two he has managed
to paint the ringing of bells.

The brush sinks.
The canvas has forced a landscape to emerge
in what merely calls itself a landscape.
And the road really turns.
Each second has a moist glint
no-one could see before.
He stands with his beating pain
in last year´s grass that is suddenly fresh.

THE OTHER LIFE

As if standing beside a burned out car
and seeing one's body crumpled over the wheel—
Today's like a normal October Saturday
but belongs to another calendar.
I seem to have groped out of my life
and stumbled into my *life*.

The same insubstantial maples and ash-trees.
The same haze with the same promises.
And the grass claims to bear our footprints.
But we've never been here before.
Digging holes for tulip bulbs you see
the earth being created beneath the spade.
While I shut off the water for winter
and hear water drip for the first time ever.

Jackdaws from an erased year
insist, insist
and persuade the field to a new attempt
still only a newly ploughed gleam.

Words like "chronology" and "explication"
are rusty tools I put in the shed.
Reason can appeal to a higher court.

The other life
with the roads we never walked
must have existed all the time
an arm's length distant
with the *sea* resounding beside the sea—
but not for him who reached out to it.
The word is grace.

The wind turns
beyond what is still smouldering

and the eyes learn that smoke can sting:
the life I didn´t choose
has suddenly chosen me.
And I am unwritten.
Write me.

THE DAY WE BURIED FOUCAULT

That inexorable black sun
has a fitting place in the calendar.
The shop grilles are of course locked—
what's one not tempted to sell today?
One is nervous too in a city
so full of streets where no-one dared to walk.
And do we know a whit about the sewage system?
The Palais de Justice is a daring hypothesis.

At the café table a German philosopher
with a moustache like a drying-up waterfall
mutters his "noch einmal" over his glass.
But whoever is looking for his other life
will have to entice an unused year
which has not been split into madness and insight.
The seventeenth century seeps out of the walls
with a convincing taste of metal.
In logic there still lives an unreasonable love.
And Paris is more than a text.

Waving gloves of misted plastic
the policeman in the middle of Boul' Mich
tries to redirect the flow of history.
The bridge too is enveloped in plastic
against saliva spray from the Seine.
Perhaps also from fear of the muttering
of this collective memory.

Admitted: our knowledge of humanity
must again be founded on hell.
The dogs stand still and listen to a cry
that passes far above the human ear—
the glass I raise to the sniffling German
shatters and cuts my hand.
He shies from the blood.

Then we´d see reason
groping on all fours
for its trampled spectacles
while madness finds refuge in its scream.
Neither has found the other.

Of course. Everything can be traced back
to the grid of knowing, to be glimpsed
even in the cracked concrete—
everything but what really happens.
Islam swept down in the gutter
floats slowly upwards.

In this infernal light one can see
how thought has been placed under wardship.
But resistance also is brought out in relief.
Each stone is a prisoner on hunger strike.

LIFE FOR SALE

The wooden fence gives up its cracked resistance
and buyers stroll in the tall grass, peeping
on tiptoe through the fly dirt on the windows.
There he sits, rooted to the kitchen table
among potato peelings and bored empties.
The shadows of his parents
try to smuggle away the food scraps
and make him sit up straight:
"He was just going to see to the nets."
But the son is unsteady as the squint privy door
that comes loose in a speculator´s hand.
He knows. Out there the trees are staggering with fruit.
But he has no longer hands to pluck it.

The dead appeal now like brokers:
"Listen, so much life in the walls,
life we hadn´t the heart to live.
And feel here with your hand—
so much knowledge round the empty calf-pen,
so much decency in the pruned trees."
Life that wants to move on, compulsorily,
and lost patience with that fellow in the kitchen
and his woman, who should have been flaunting her belly.

Of course he hears, the lignified farmer,
how stairway and out-house haggle.
But can´t be bothered butting in.
Breathing, after all, costs 13%.
And the treachery is completed.
The pump and the barn have turned their backs on him
and smirk ingratiatingly
at whoever is most likely to bid highest.
The gossip of the centuries in the walls
agrees to every conceivable latex-paint
and centuries of footsteps are ready for the sander.

The dead come to meet the newcomers
and try to breathe with their lungs.

That fellow at what was recently a table
is so abandoned by the things in the farmyard
he can no longer catch sight of the fireplace.
Even the food scraps and last year's newspaper
move off away from him
towards a new attempt.

CARIBBEAN QUARTET

1.
This copper engraving from 1900
has burns and curled edges
as if about to break into flame.
But the frigate bird soars out of the paper
and in again, draws away, comes back
irrespective of what the picture is aware of.
No, the eruption has not yet happened.
At the same time the volcano is erupting.
And Saint-Pierre with its human mass,
with ships, chickens and fluttering clothes-lines
is in the midst of its luxuriating life
buried in horror and pumice.
A lady in black with an umbrella
held up against the rain of fire
is just alighting from a mule-drawn tram—
she has all the time in the world
although the rails are already bent by the heat.
"It´s only me who knows," cries the paperboy,
this cavity in the lava.

Thought is captive in the engraved pattern.
The leap belongs to philosophy.
And the only one free
is the prisoner behind a metre-thick wall
sleeping himself sober while time melts.

Clad in amazed mercy
he´ll be exhibited in the cities of Europe
as the man who survived history.
People will finger and measure and photograph
this inconceivable other life.

The real prisoners throng outside the prison-bars
among the merciless lines of the engraving,

laughing, calling, inside the stone.

Outside the peep-hole a handsbreadth of sky
and a fraction of a second:
the frigate bird.

2.
Caribbean rain:
like falling mightily in love
with the one you´ve loved for long—
suddenly I´m standing in the dark.
The rain smoothes out my features
and washes out my eye-holes,
beats right through my rib-cage
and drums on my pelvis
that steams in helpless confusion.
There are no words.
The rain on fossil lips
makes language obsolete.
An invasion to be read as liberation.
In full sunlight this darkness
which can´t exist but does.
And that is the first day of creation.

3.
You who are close as sweat on the forehead
but live in another fold of time:
hold us—so we´re not snatched by the wind
and scattered among the centuries.
You who tend the fields by night
with inward-gazing eyes
and faint smiles that know the way,
you who mend the broken fences
and prevent misfortune while we sleep,
you who polish the words while waiting for dawn:
don´t lose patience with us.
Without you bread would not be bread,

without you the ground would be friable as sugar,
without you language would turn its back on us.
Your death turns our life into life.
Hold us tight with your chilled hands.

4.
I open the shutters with stiff fingers:
for someone who has slept in a monument
it is hard to break free of the stone.
A changeling city. Old Havanna
turns its worn face to the sea
and daren´t show its teeth in a smile.

"The Revolution Continues!" shout the posters.
In the cracked glue beneath them
we can read the lower revolution
the one that makes the dictator drop his glance
in case other eyes will steal his strength.
"The world may sink," his fist says,
"if only I can define the ending."
The loudspeakers multiply in the trees.

The blockade is now in its hundredth year.
The people are living on beans and air
and the bitter drink of experience.
No thought can be thought to a conclusion.
The street-lamp also adds to the darkness.

Once the capital was moved here.
Now they´ve moved the concept of man
to the shrinking area within the walls.
The forbidden city outside
is populated by sceptical shadows
who´ve seen too much and are called the dead.

Boys who are only sketches for boys
and in the meantime live between the stones

prowl hungrily round the visitors
to snatch their language and experience.
And the threadbare war ministry
retrains as a museum
without the guards noticing.

I've stopped short before a bad painting
of a memorial service in 1828
with the gentlefolk in blue and white Empire style
and the populace like clinging apes behind the fence—
masters like slaves trapped in the pattern.
I myself am trapped in another pattern,
held together by stiffening thoughts.
But in mid-afternoon a crack opens
for another freedom than Freedom:
a woman in the picture looks this way sidelong
and her glance sinks in mine.
Only seconds separate us.

The frigate bird soars out of her time
into mine
and back into hers.

LETTER WRITING

1.
Half the letter is written
by the person it is sent to.
You, waiting for my lines—
there's so much you already know about me
that I am too close to see.
So much you can tell me
through my scribbling hand.
From the paper before me there rises
a murmuring like the noise
from headphones laid aside.

2.
I wrote to Nichita Stanescu
not knowing he'd just died.
Felt an alien chill rising
from the writing up through my hand.
Such a lack of sense-impressions in the room!
I forced his image to appear in the wall-paper:
his puffed features which had learned too much,
the smile where the poem had vanished,
the feet that had given notice to the shoes.
But the frost rose up my arm.
The frozen words on the page
repelled their meaning.
Halfway through, the letter was over.

3.
So much wiser the writing
than the writer.
These lines become more and more oblique
and the message altered into something
neither of us intended.
The last part will maybe break loose
and describe something beyond both of us—
our turned-away history, so valid
that our faces dare to leave us.

FAMILY MEMORY

When the blind war was over
a farmer from Red Island was condemned
to block and wheel
for the crime of hailing the king that lost.

His wife walked from Jämtland to beg
mercy from the proper Majesty.
With shrinking heart and bleeding feet
she reached Stockholm in time.
Stopped the king at the city gate,
her hand on the stirrup: "Gracious Lord—"
And His Magnificence, the sun into his breast
as the horse reared, was pleased
to grant her her husband's head
in confirmation thereof setting
a stern seal on the bill of pardon.

With steps that dared to love again
she turned back north.
But arriving at last
after stony weeks she found
no boat on her side of the strait.
Everyone had crossed the water
to see how it fares with a man
from whom God has turned His face.
And so she stood with rigid lips
on the mainland shore and saw
in the distance her husband's head fall.

ARCHETYPE

The picture in the cave
has been lifted into the paper:
Chinese monk rides a fish
as big as a boat.
Outstretched leaves on his bamboo staff
depict the speed. His eyes and mouth
are opened wide by the water's resistance.
But the figure itself is stillness
and the bridle in his hand invisible:
he rides as if he weren't riding.
Both are red, the monk an assemblage
of leathery doctrines
he smilingly disclaims,
the fish a fusion of scales and surprise
—the round eye knows it belongs
to a lower realm of horror and madness.
So together they manage to transform
the white world around them:
bubbles, creases, beginnings,
already emerging from the frame.

DIDN´T YOU TELL ME A DREAM

Didn´t you tell me a dream
about standing in a night without stars,
looking in through the window
at me and the children round the table,
unable to give us a sign?
None of us could have thought
that I should be the first to end up in darkness.

I´m now standing outside the house
which came to us too late in life
and gaze and gaze at you through the window,
but I can´t see the person you´re talking to.
Your words that kept me alive
have clearly gone astray today.
I´m helpless like an empty battery.

But then look up for Christ´s sake—
I´m giving you sign after sign,
signs with power to reach you
only one moment more.
But you´re staring at someone I can´t see.
And I realize I´m dead.

I KNEW THAT PHOTOS FADED

I knew that photos faded
when long exposed to...was it called "sun"?
What I didn't know
was that existence is fading, day by day,
for those given a respite like me.
Soon a year must have passed.
Anyway heaven and trees have whitened.
Your face is transparent,
your words have gone thin
and your hand, the half of a hand
which couldn't be severed from mine
is so white I can barely see it.
Is it because you follow me
into what can't be seen?
Or is it because I am slowly
losing sight of you?

HOLD ME TIGHT SO I DO NOT FLEE

Hold me tight so I do not flee.
Something is forcing me away. I´m astray
in the dusk, no, it isn´t dusk—
more a lack of meaning,
along a meandering, dusty road.
It looks like the road between village and church
but it is no road
and here is neither village nor church.
The one thing I know is the wandering
takes me further and further away from you.
Only your words,
only a language that knows me,
knows every thought and fear,
can seize my straying soul by the hand
and drag me back into what exists.

I can´t see what forces me away.
But it seems stronger than your thoughts.
And I´m forced further and further into the silence
along what I took for a road.
Your words feel so distant.
Hold me fast. I flee.

VITA NUOVA

Starting to build on the seventh floor,
with air underneath, may inspire misgivings.
The removal firm must hire a crane.
We agree after all the foundation is good.
And we aren´t the first to lose our lives.

Vita nuova. Noch einmal.
You search a caption for a new existence
that recalls everything but has nothing left.
Every word is a diary filled with scribbling.
Every word is blank, awaiting a voice.

The worn wooden floor is new
and holds our weight though it floats.
Thin figures crossing the rooms
claim their right to speak.
Let them talk. We can afford it.
It´s the lift that is a case for the censor.

A finished life meeting a finished life:
shall we take your shameless brown dining-table
or my well-worn white?

Before the lamp there´s yet its circle of light.
Like your smile anticipating me.
Like my thoughts beginning in yours.

One could no doubt have expected the screech
of a lorry waved in by the Customs
or possibly the thud of metal against wood
when the skipper was too hasty at the pier.
Hardly these bars by Schubert.
Hardly these experienced words,
calmly awaiting their meaning.

IF EVEN DENIED A MAYFLY´S HOUR

If even denied a mayfly´s hour,
yes, if granted only a single minute
we must make that minute our life.
Not much of a world is needed—
a soughing of trees would suffice.
But you would be close.
The hand I´d lifted towards your face
would know nothing, as yet.
Our temples would throb,
our lips would stiffen.
And we would check ourselves like that
for the whole of our long minute.

SILENCE

For Tomas Tranströmer

As if silence itself had meant to alert me.
I walked along the beach, the sea was quarrelsome
and tossed up a heap of shingle.
The rasp of withdrawal, like a landslide.
I didn't catch what it meant.

One day an absent-minded finger
was stuck from nowhere into my head.
Like stopping the hand of a grandfather clock
and taking the language back to just after one.

She had sensed that rasping within me
and cried: "You are too tired. Don´t go!"
But my brief-case insisted, bulging with duties.
I seized my coat and reached the door
before the landslide took me.

Once I lifted a century of seas
in my dripping hand. Like the spy
miniaturising his photo of the deployment plan
and fitting it into an o in a letter.

It´s getting dark. The spruce trees blacken
like the pages of my calendar. But turn the pages
and let the blackness light your way.

Yes, I usually speak in a borrowed voice,
the voice of the woman who reads in me
translating my Swedish into Swedish.
Like pressing oneself through a keyhole
and almost getting shoulders and hips through it.

So many forestalling my life in theirs.
The thumb in the air at the roadside
made my language brake and pick them up.
Like this paralysed composer
with his Russian like glue in his mouth
but music from his eyes and his step.

After all I myself anticipated:
an axe-blow from within flares up
so intensely it´s seen for years in advance.
I could therefore in time
send out four lines
to search for the meaning of the deceit.
The night of the black day they were back
and what they brought was calm.

Thus the final chapter insists. My rocking-chair
is rocking in dogged iambs,
a resignation that won't give in.

Now I´m being completed like a text
to music that is half turned away
but existed for long and knows me well.
History is scrawled as before between the lines,
lines which do not know where they´re going.
The handwriting
looks like my old Latin teacher´s.

So at last I taught
silence itself to speak.

from **VINTERGATA /
LEND ME YOUR VOICE**
(2007)

INTRODUCTION

Imagine moments when all the experience and all the values of a human being are condensed into a sudden insight. The universe of time surrounding you might then glitter like a milky way from such epiphanies—sometimes ecstatic, more often bitter but always with the lustre of human understanding. If we managed to catch these testimonies, how would they sound? It is the poet's task to answer that question. It is a challenge I once expressed in a poem: "Lend me your voice!" The moments which could be recreated in that way form a series without an end, a history on the margin of History.

A similar catalogue was begun more than two thousand years ago by the anonymous Greek poets who gave voice to the many dead in the work known as *The Greek Anthology*.

Although an ice-block has saved me for your time
you can't reach me.
You ask, Who were you?
What did you think? Who did you love?
Just what I ask myself.
You know only my last meal:
dried goat's meat and nuts.
The last thing I ate though was probably snow.
Beaten by the storm, fingers and feet numb,
all I remember happening was:
a woman stooping over me
where I lay crouched on the path—
a stranger I thought I'd always known.
I fumbled right through her.
Her face was burning, out of reach.
She stayed with me
while the world shrank to an ice-block.

The air smells of approaching thunder.
Are we still in the age of wars?
Are new heads being spiked up on stakes
in the rubbish dumps beyond the city gate?
I know only this moment:
pressed together like two dragonflies
we soar out across the Euphrates, buzzing,
filled by something resembling sunlight.

I was standing in front of Anubis,
a simple Egyptian merchant,
to have my heart weighed.
On the other pan lay a feather.
If my heart was heavier, I was lost.
Only a heart without stone
gains admittance to the ultimate.
With tears streaming
down my decomposed face I watched
how the pan with the chicken-feather sank.

It was plague month in Athens.
The sick threw themselves in wells
to get a moment of coolness
and relieve their annihilating thirst.
We doctors were helpless.
The dying appealed to me
with voices harsh from their blistered throats.
Their mouths already stank of corpse.
I did what little I could,
cooled them with wet cloths
and moistened the blackened lips.
I allowed the spasms to enter me
and the cold to rise from my feet.
When the sick gouged out their eyes
their despair was mine.

When I had stopped breathing
I could feel how you looked at me
and your heart slackened its pace—
you suddenly found me that beautiful.
I could read in your thoughts
you'd go straight to the stonemason
so he could recreate me,
smiling, leaning on an elbow
along the lid of my sarcophagus.
But don't imagine me as stone yet!
That prevented you now from noticing
how my eyelids winced.
They tried to overcome the stone
which had already found its way into them.
I wanted to open my eyes
and see you once again.

It must have been a hall
with a window at each end,
each giving on nothing.
A swallow flickered in through the one,
swirled about dazzled by light
and vanished through the other.
I can see that was my life
but not who I was.
Perhaps a Saxon chieftain
struck by the sudden brightness
into believing it was God he'd met
and now perforce must christen his people.
Or perhaps an Arabian poet
presented with his life's work
in a moment suffused with light
between nothing and nothing.

My horsemen had conquered the world.
I could raise a wall of skulls,
claim any woman my eye fell upon.
No-one looked me in the eye any more.
Yet I was consumed by envy
of the scrofulous old man I rode down.
To dry the sweat of my brow
after a day in the rice-paddies.
To stroke the back of my ox
and look into its experienced eyes.
To feel the evening chill round my legs
on my way home, stooped under firewood.

I was called Maria. I was made of wood,
a wooden sorrow, long-drawn-out
wooden thoughts, a worn-out wooden womb.
But my robe shone with lapis lazuli
and was bespangled with pin-point stars.
Once I was cajoled into smiling
by a jester who wanted to honour
The Mother of God with his meagre skills.
He did somersaults, sang in falsetto,
mimicked all of nature's creatures,
was so pathetic even wood could feel touched.
I stepped down from my plinth,
my robe a billowing aurora,
and held the startled fellow's head
in my hands. Dazed by his smells
I fumbled in his matted hair,
stooped, creaking,
kissed his sweaty forehead.
At that an unkown pain stabbed me—
I was, for a moment, human.
I fled back up on my plinth
leaving the jester shaken
by what he took to be a miracle.
But the real amazement, the miracle
of humanity - that was mine.

In the minutes before they fetched me
I stood by the window, forehead on the glass.
The rattle of the prisoner's cart on the cobbles,
the boos and gobbets of the mob,
the drums surrounding the guillotine—
none of these yet existed.
Calmy I took leave of the voices in the street
through the reflection of my pocked face.
Nodded at the passers-by, at my wards
who smiled back without suspecting
I would that day be called a traitor.
I had to lean on the window-frame
taking leave too of the revolution
soon to be sold to the highest bidder.
I gazed wistfully at the cloud:
it carried my dream beyond the reach
of those who booted their way up my stairs.

As in earlier years
when I'd been heavily thrashed
I took my way down to the river
to let my gaze follow its flow
and teach myself indifference.
But this evening
the Volga bore a film of sunlight
with the gold of molten tin in a crucible.
Lord,
how can you let a tormented serf
witness a beauty that gives such pain?

We'd been driven in chains along the paths
for more days than the hand has fingers.
Then the world widened between the trees
in din and dazzle that shrank the heart.
Terrified at the ship out there
I stumbled on a root and fell
face down in the mud.
Then an iron-heeled boot stamped my neck
with all the weight of the slave-driver
and I was cursed in a language
as white and hard as the bones of the dead.
I caught a hint of the bitter story
they planned to engrave on my back.

Driving my load across the ice
I heard the ice crack—a floe slanted
sliding me into the water.
The load went down, the horse went up,
kicking at the air
to pull us up among the clouds.
Then the green lid of ice
shut over us.
The questions swarmed round me:
all those worries I pestered the priest with,
the tattered books,
margins scribbled with my anxieties.
They never found us.
But in the rising bubbles I saw clearly
what life had wanted of me.

All I owned was a sledge-hammer.
The cliff jutting into the ocean
found no takers so I was free
to break it up, first into splinters,
day after day after day,
then into dust to mix with seaweed.
I begged potatoes and planted them
in the soil I'd forced from the sea.
But my greatest conquest was a face
sweeter than potato blossom
and a voice that set my groin on fire.
We rejoiced together in the harvest.
That was the year before the potato blight
and death along all the roads.

I think I took to preaching,
left land and family.
I know only I was wakened
by the byre in flames
and the cattle bleating and bellowing.
I rushed over with buckets
but the thatch was already all in flames,
speaking to me in a blazing voice.
I fell on my knees, begged for mercy.
And all at once the flames were out.
The cattle calmly chewed the cud
and stared at me with wondering eyes.
All as it had been, yet all changed
after the visitation
of the voice that speaks through fire.

One of a swarm he leapt at the trench
grey in the grey like Ypres itself,
struck my rifle aside with a roar
I recognized, powerless to resist.
I caught only one insight,
as in the sheen of a flare:
our leaders have duped us!
When he twisted his bayonette in my breast
—I didn't even manage to feel pain—
I saw his face, wrenched by fear.
That face was my own.

I stooped along the dark passage,
one of us small Philippinos trained
for close combat in narrow confines,
flown here to Vietnam
and put into the tunnel system of Cu Chi.
Suddenly someone breathing in the dark,
an arm's length ahead of me.
A click from a safety-catch.
And my own finger's on the trigger.
We wait and wait and wait.
The one is thinking in the other:
if only both of us draw back
one of us won't die.
The past of both of us is gathered here,
mother's prayers, village school,
attempted love,
all like a smell of sweat in a smell of sweat.
The moment gets longer and longer.
Breath draws through breath.

An arrested moment in a garden—
that's all there is.
This white foam must be a bird-cherry in bloom,
sudden like desire.
The blackbird screws its song in further.
Your gaze is fathomless.
And the trees have lifted,
earth spilling from their roots,
lifted like your rapturous gaze
a moment before it subsides.

Lying in my cell
with a sliver of light
and a stinking bucket
as the last remnants of reality
I found out it was my best friend
who'd betrayed me—
and my wife had given them "evidence."
The torturers turned me inside out like a sock
to make me confess.
Then I saw the horror in their eyes—
they felt, like a sudden breath of wind,
how history turned its back on them.

On that day the gods took the shape
of a band of Serbian peasant boys
who manned their hill-top artillery,
taking revenge for all that lack of respect.
Fleering, they fired shell upon shell
on us hated townsfolk in the valley.
Others will tell you
about the sight that met me
when the grenade caught my children.
I couldn't even cry
since my eyes were at once stones.
Time moved more and more slowly.
Instead of sorrow, stone filled my veins,
reaching into fingers and feet.
Here I am now, a statue of sorrow
I can't myself feel.
My eyes in the rock observe the new life
without observing. I am aware only
of the playful spite of the gods.

Before sinking onto the bench
I managed to see how the strait
was an unwritten page, without a ripple
but with a collar of overnight ice.
A last sign, perhaps an abandoned heron,
tall at the water's edge, had something to tell me.
All the answer my heart had was a cramp.
If the other side exists
somewhere in the haze
it's like a presentiment of tree-tops,
more an uncertain promise than leaves.
The age of men is clearly past.
I would have liked to meet them.

About the Author

Kjell Espmark (b. 1930) is a poet, novelist, and literary historian. He is also former professor in Comparative Literature at the University of Stockholm. Since 1981 he is a member of the Swedish Academy, and since 1988 a member also of its Nobel Committee (chairman 1988-2004). He has been awarded a considerable number of prizes, including the Bellman Prize (for poetry) and the Schück Prize (for literary criticism). Latest awards: The Kellgren Prize, The Great Prize of De Nio ("The Nine"), and the Tranströmer Prize. He is an officer of L´Ordre de Mérite.

Espmark has published thirteen volumes of poetry. One of them—*När vägen vänder*—can be read in English: *Route Tournante* (translation Joan Tate, Forest Books, London & Boston 1993); selections are to be found in *Béla Bartók against the Third Reich* (Oasis/Shearsman, London 1985), *Four Swedish Poets* (White Pine Press, Fredonia, New York 1990), and *Five Swedish Poets* (Norvik Press, Norwich 1997), all in Robin Fulton Macpherson's translation. A selection can be read in Spanish translation by Francisco J. Uriz: *Voces sin tumba* (Fundación Jorge Guillén, Valladolid 2005). Espmark´s latest book of poetry, *Vintergata* (2007), has appeared in English as *Lend Me Your Voice*, translation by Robin Fulton Macpherson (Marick Press, 2011) and in Spanish as *Via láctea*, translation by Francisco J. Uriz (Prames, Madrid 2009). A German version has the title *vintergata/milchstrasse*, translation Klaus-Juergen Liedtke (Kleinheinrich, Muenster 2011). Also versions in Italian, Chinese, Arabic, Croatian, and Icelandic have appeared. His collected poetry 1956-2009 has recently been published with the title *Det enda nödvändiga* (literally: "The only necessary", 2010). Espmark´s poetry has been translated into some twenty languages.

Espmark has also published a series of novels, called *Glömskans tid* (*The Age of Oblivion*, seven vols 1987-97, in one volume 1999). The first volume is available in French (*L´Oubli*, Gallimard, Paris 1990), Italian, and Romanian, the fifth in French (*La Haine/L'Oubli*, Michael de Maule, Paris, 2011). His novel *Voltaires resa* (Voltaire´s Journey, 2000) has appeared in French (*Le voyage de Voltaire*, Actes Sud, 2006), Dutch and Romanian. His novel *Béla Bartók mot Tredje riket* (Béla Bartók against the Third Reich, 2004) has been published in French (*Béla Bartók contre le troisième Reich*, Actes Sud, 2006), Spanish (*Béla Bartók contra el tercer Reich*, Bassarai, Vitoria-Gasteiz, 2007), and Romanian. His book *Motvilliga historier* (Reluctant stories, 2006) can be read in French (*Histoires à contrecœur*, Actes Sud).

Espmark´s ten books of literary criticism include studies of Artur Lundkvist, Harry Martinson, Tomas Tranströmer, and a redefinition of the Modernist tradition from Baudelaire to our days: *Att översätta själen* (Translating the Soul, 1975), His best-known work of criticism is *The Nobel Prize in Literature, A Study of the Criteria behind the Choices*, first published in 1986 and later appearing in several languages; an English version was published in 1991 (G.K.Hall & Co., Boston). The book appeared in a thoroughly revised and updated version as *Litteraturpriset, Hundra år med Nobel´s uppdrag* (The Literary Prize, A Hundred Years with Nobel´s Assignment, 2001*)*. It has been published in many countries, most recently in a Spanish version (*El premio Nobel de Literatura, Cien años con la misión*, Nórdica libros, Madrid 2008).

www.ingramcontent.com/pod-product-compliance
Lightning Source LLC
LaVergne TN
LVHW011423080426
835512LV00005B/229